Discovering Cultures

Colombia

Sarah De Capua

MARSHALL CAVENDISH
NEW YORK

Benchmark Books
Marshall Cavendish
99 White Plains Road
Tarrytown, New York 10591-9001
www.marshallcavendish.com

Library of Congress Cataloging-in-Publication Data

De Capua, Sarah.
Colombia / by Sarah De Capua.
p. cm. — (Discovering cultures)
Summary: Highlights the geography, people, food, schools, recreation, celebrations, and language of Colombia.
Includes bibliographical references and index.
ISBN 0-7614-1715-X
1. Colombia—Juvenile literature. [1. Colombia.] I. Title. II. Series.
F2258.5.D42 2003
986.1—dc21   2003008128

Photo Research by Candlepants Incorporated

Cover Photo: Jeremy Horner / *Corbis*

The photographs in this book are used by permission and through the courtesy of: *Victor Englebert*: 1, 4, 6, 11, 14, 15, 17, 20-21, 27, 28, 30, 31 (lower), 34, 35, 37, 43 (lower right), back cover. *Corbis*: Enzo & Paolo Ragazzini, 7, 16, 42; Ted Speigel, 8; Kevin Schafer, 9; David Reed, 10; Sergio Pitamitz, 12-13, 43 (top left); Carl & Ann Purcell, 18, 19; Jan Butchofsky-Houser, 24; Richard Bickle, 26; AFP, 31 (top); Diego Lezama Orezzoli, 32, 43 (lower left); Jeremy Horner, 36, 38; Richard Schulman 44. *Envision*: Steven Needham, 22; Madeline Polss, 23. *Art Archive/Museo 20 de Julio de 1810 Bogata/Dagli Orti*: 44.

Cover: *San Pedro Claver Church, Colombia*; Title page: *A young Colombian girl*

Map and illustrations by Ian Warpole
Book design by Virginia Pope

Printed in China
1 3 5 6 4 2

Turn the Pages...

Where in the World Is Colombia?

Colombia is one of the largest countries in South America. It lies in the north-western part of the *continent*. Two oceans touch Colombia's shores. The Caribbean Sea is to the northwest. The Pacific Ocean lies to the southwest.

Colombia's neighbors include four South American countries: Venezuela, Brazil, Peru, and Ecuador. Colombia is also neighbors with Panama, a Central American country. Since Colombia borders both Central and South America, it is often called the Gateway to South America.

Colombia's Caribbean coast

Map of Colombia

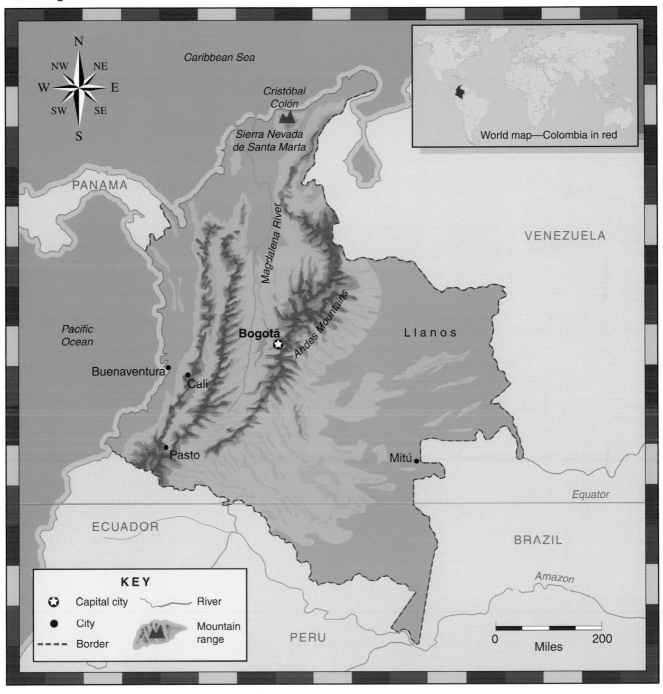

Caribbean Sea

Cristóbal Colón

Sierra Nevada de Santa Marta

PANAMA

Magdalena River

Pacific Ocean

Bogotá

Andes Mountains

Llanos

VENEZUELA

Buenaventura

Cali

Pasto

Mitú

ECUADOR

Equator

BRAZIL

Amazon

PERU

World map—Colombia in red

KEY

⬡ Capital city   River

● City   Mountain range

---- Border

0   Miles   200

The Pacific islands of Malpelo and Gorgona are also part of Colombia. So are San Andrés, Providencia, and other smaller islands in the Caribbean Sea.

Huge mountains rise high into the sky from Colombia. They are known as the Andes. Like most mountains, the Andes are part of long lines of mountains called mountain ranges. Three Andes mountain ranges lie side by side in Colombia. They are the Cordillera Occidental (western), the Cordillera Central, and the Cordillera Oriental (eastern). Between the Cordillera Central and Cordillera Oriental is the Magdalena River. It is the most important river in the country.

Between the mountain ranges are river valleys where food is grown. Many people live in these valleys. Bogotá is Colombia's capital city. It is in the Cordillera Oriental. Bogotá is home to more than five million people.

The Andes Mountains rise higher than the clouds over Colombia.

Bogotá, Colombia's capital city

Along the Caribbean Sea in northern Colombia are the Caribbean lowlands. Here huge ships load and unload goods at the country's largest *ports*. A mountain range called Sierra Nevada de Santa Marta is in the northern part of this region. Colombia's highest mountains are in this mountain range. Cristóbal Colón is the highest peak in the country. Its name is Spanish for Christopher Columbus. It stands 18,947 feet (5,775 meters) high.

The Pacific lowlands are along the southwestern coast. They lie between the ocean and the Cordillera Occidental. The largest city here is Buenaventura.

Cattle grazing on the llanos

Eastern Colombia is mostly large and flat. This area is known as the *llanos* (plains). The llanos are not good for growing crops. They are used mainly for grazing cattle. The llanos make up most of Colombia, but few Colombians live there.

The rain forest is south of the llanos. This hot, humid region is home to some of Colombia's Indians. Many kinds of birds and animals live in the Colombian rain forest. Only the rain forests of Brazil have more.

Colombia is located close to the *equator*. This means its climate, or weather, does not change much. The climate of an area depends on its height above sea level. The higher you are above sea level, the colder it gets.

There are really only two seasons in Colombia. The dry season is from December to March. It returns from July to September. The rainy season is from October to November, and then again from April to June.

The Capybara

Do you know the name of the world's largest rodent? It is the capybara. Rodents are mammals. This means they have hair, are warm-blooded, and nurse their young with mother's milk. Rodents are easy to spot. They have two large front teeth for gnawing. Other examples of rodents are rats, mice, and squirrels.

Capybaras live in the watery areas of Colombia's llanos. They are usually 3 to 4 feet (about 1 meter) long, about the size of a pig. Capybaras have webbed feet, which helps them swim. When swimming, only the eyes, ears, and nostrils show above the water. Capybaras live in family groups and eat plants.

It is common in Colombia for *gauchos* (cowboys) to catch capybaras by lassoing them like cattle. Capybara meat is especially popular at Easter.

What Makes Colombia Colombian?

Many different groups of people call Colombia home. More than 40 million people live in Colombia, mostly in the mountains.

Colombians have mixed backgrounds. They may be Spanish, Indian, African, or European. Most Colombians are *mestizos*. Mestizos are people who are both Spanish and Indian. The second-largest group is Spanish. Mulattoes are those who are both Spanish and African. They make up the third-largest part of the population.

Colombian children in Bogotá

Some people are African or Colombian Indian. Others are both African and Indian. This is the smallest group in Colombia. They are known as *zambos*.

Indians live mostly in the mountains. Many have become part of the modern Colombian community. However, some Indians have kept their traditional way of life. Colombia's Indians include the Kogi, the Paez, and the Guambiano.

Spanish is Colombia's official language. Indians speak their native languages. English is spoken on the Caribbean islands of San Andrés and Providencia. English is also spoken in Colombia's large cities, including Bogotá, Medellín, and Cali.

Most Colombians are Roman Catholic. Catholicism is the country's official religion. Some Colombians practice a mixture of Catholicism

A rain forest Indian wearing traditional handmade jewelry

and Indian or African religions. Many Indians follow their traditional religions. There are also small numbers of Jews and Protestants in Colombia.

Most people in Colombia's large cities dress like people in North America. Men wear suits to work. Women wear dresses and suits. Outside the cities, jeans and T-shirts are common.

Many people can be seen wearing a *ruana*. A ruana is a wool wrap that is pulled over the head. Some Colombians wear their ruanas folded over one shoulder. Men, women, and children also wear hats that are round on top with a narrow brim. These hats protect them from the sun.

Colombian Indians may wear traditional clothing. Indians in the mountains wear loose cotton pants and shirts. Rain forest Indians wear very little clothing because it is so hot.

Colombian music comes from the many groups that make up the country.

Roman Catholic churches can be found throughout the country.

A Colombian Indian weaving a basket

Indians make music with drums and flutes made of bamboo. *Cumbia* music has African roots. *Bambuco* and *torbellino* music combine Spanish and Indian rhythms. Colombians also enjoy music from outside the country. Salsa comes from the Caribbean. Tango is from Argentina. Colombians enjoy music, dancing, and singing at festivals, in restaurants, and in parks.

Colombians have been creating traditional crafts since before Columbus arrived in the late 1400s. Bamboo, cactus, and palm are used to make strong, beautiful baskets. They can be used to carry food and supplies. Some Indians

This woman is weaving a hammock.

weave baskets so tightly that they can hold water! Cloth weaving is also a traditional craft. Ruanas are examples of woven cloth. Pottery is made throughout Colombia. Some pots are painted in different colors. Others are made from red and black clay. Many visitors to Colombia take home baskets, cloth, and pottery as souvenirs.

Coffee plants grow on steep mountainsides.

Do you know an adult who enjoys drinking Colombian coffee? It is believed to be one of the most delicious coffees in the world. Coffee beans are grown on small farms high in the mountains. Other important products are sugarcane and soybeans. Fruits such as bananas, oranges, and papayas are also popular. All of these products are shipped to other countries, including the United States. The next time you go to the grocery store, look to see if any of the fruit was grown in Colombia.

Glittering Gold

When the Spanish arrived in Colombia in the early 1500s, the Indians told them a legend about *El Dorado* (The Golden Man). The Spanish thought El Dorado was a city made of gold. More Spanish explorers came to Colombia in search of the golden city. They found Indians using golden fishhooks, needles, helmets, cups, and dishes. This made the Spanish search even harder for El Dorado.

El Dorado was never found, but today a huge collection of gold *artifacts* can be seen in the Gold Museum in Bogotá. The museum has more than 35,000 gold objects that were made before Columbus arrived. They include spoons, bowls, and jewelry, such as nose rings and bracelets. The museum's gold collection is the largest in South America.

Living in Colombia

Most Colombians live in the cities. They work as bankers, business owners, government workers, and teachers. Some have jobs in factories making chemicals or tires. Many people live in small brick houses or apartment buildings. The buildings look like apartment buildings in North America. They are tall, shiny, and modern.

More people move to Colombia's cities every year. However, there are not enough houses, schools, and jobs for everyone. As a result, many Colombians are poor. Their homes are dirty shacks on the edges of the cities. Usually they have no electricity or running water. The Colombian government does not want so many of their people to be poor. Leaders are working to provide the people with more education and job opportunities.

Rich Colombian families live in beautiful neighborhoods. Their large homes

Tall apartment buildings in Bogotá

A small farmhouse in a mountain village

often include flowering gardens and a swimming pool. Outside the cities, people live mostly in towns and villages and work on small farms. In some mountain towns, houses are made of mud or stone. They are usually one or two stories tall. All of the rooms inside open onto a *courtyard*. Beautiful, sweet-smelling plants and flowers fill the courtyard. This is where the family comes together to eat and to relax.

Fishing villages line the Caribbean and Pacific coasts. Banana *plantations* are found nearby. On the llanos, where few people live, cattle graze and grain grows. Gauchos ride on horseback to keep track of the cattle herds.

The homes of Indians who live in the rain forests are platforms covered with *thatched* roofs. Many Indians in the cool mountains live in huts made of wood and straw. They hunt and fish for food for their families.

Whether rich or poor, family life is important to all Colombians. Grandparents, parents, children, and sometimes aunts and uncles live together in one home. Colombian children remain close to their parents throughout their lives. They usually live in their parents' home until they get married. Colombian families enjoy spending time together—at parks, playing games or sports, and at mealtimes.

Huts with thatched roofs in an Indian village in the Andes

Empanadas are a delicious meal.

Lunch is the most important meal of the day. It may take two hours to complete! This meal usually begins with beef or chicken soup. Along the coasts, the soup is made with seafood. Next comes the main dish of beef or pork. Rice or potatoes, as well as vegetables, are served with the meat. *Arepas* are cornmeal pancakes that are a popular part of the main meal. They are eaten with breakfast and during the smaller evening meal as well. Arepas are cut in half like muffins. They can be buttered or filled with cheese, meat, or vegetables.

Empanadas and *tamales* are also a main meal. Empanadas are pastry turnovers that are filled with

Tamales may be served with salsa and guacamole.

beef. Tamales are banana leaves wrapped around a mixture of pork, potatoes, eggs, and vegetables. They are cooked by using steam or boiling water.

Many different kinds of fruit grow in Colombia. People use them to make popular drinks called *jugos*. Jugos can be made from the juice of pineapples, mangoes, and nectarines, or from Colombian fruits called *maracuya* and *curuba*. These refreshing drinks are enjoyed year-round.

A woman carries and sells fruit in Cartagena.

Let's Eat!
Jugo

Ask an adult to help you make this tasty fresh-fruit drink.

Ingredients:

1 nectarine or peach,
cut in chunks

$1/2$ cup milk

$1/2$ cup orange juice

1 tablespoon honey

$1/4$ teaspoon almond extract

2 ice cubes, crushed

Wash your hands. Put all of the ingredients in a blender. Blend at high speed for 15 seconds. Makes 1 $1/2$ cups, or one serving.

School Days

Today, most Colombians are able to read and write. Public schools in Colombia are free to all children. Parents who can afford it send their children to private schools. Many of these schools are run by the Catholic Church. Students at private schools wear uniforms—shirts with vests or jackets and pants for boys and skirts for girls. The uniforms are similar to those worn by schoolchildren in North America.

All Colombian children between the ages of six and fourteen must attend school. Some children younger than six attend preschool. Primary school is for children ages six to fourteen. Students who do well in primary school can go to high school. Most high schools are located in cities. This makes it difficult for children in the country to attend high school. Students who do well in high school might go on to universities. Like high schools, most universities are found in large cities.

The school year begins in February and continues

Colombian schoolchildren

Many classrooms have blackboards, just like classrooms in North America.

until the end of June. From the end of June until the middle of July, there is a two-week vacation. When it is over, students head back to school until the middle of November. Students have a long vacation from then until the next school year starts in February.

The school day begins at 7:30 A.M. It ends in the early afternoon. Students spend the rest of the day doing homework, after-school activities, or sports. The school week is five days long, from Monday to Friday. In addition to the weekends and school vacations, students have time off for national holidays.

A music class in the city of Cali

Colombian students study history, math, science, social studies, and Spanish. English is taught in some primary schools and most high schools. They also study dance, music, and theater. Once each month, students attend an *assembly* at which they honor their country. They say the pledge of allegiance to the Colombian flag and sing the national anthem.

Outside the city, not as many children go to school. Sometimes their parents need them to work to help support the family. Other children do not go to school because the nearest school building may be many miles away. There are no school buses to take them to school, and many families do not own cars.

In the rain forest, some Indian children have classes similar to those in traditional schools. Most, however, have a very different kind of learning. They learn from their parents and the adults in their community. They watch them hunt, fish, make medicine from plants, prepare food, or make a thatched roof. After watching adults, young Indians learn by copying them.

The Monkey People

Colombian children enjoy a folktale called "The Monkey People."
In this story, the villagers in an Amazon rain forest become lazy. They complain about all the chores they have to do, so they stop doing them. Every time their village gets dirty, they move to a new one. After a while, even moving becomes too much trouble for them.

One day, a little boy brings a mysterious old man to the village. The old man carves monkeys out of leaves. He offers to bring the leaf monkeys to life for the villagers. The people happily agree. At first, the villagers ask the monkeys to do their daily chores for them. In spite of the monkeys' help, the villagers continue to complain. They become more and more lazy. Eventually the villagers ask the monkeys to do everything for them—even to breathe for them! Soon it is hard to tell who are the humans and who are the monkeys.

Colombian children enjoy this folktale because they like the idea of getting monkeys to do their chores. Grown-ups enjoy its important lessons about the dangers of laziness and why it is important to avoid complaining all the time.

Just for Fun

Colombian children enjoy their free time. They play games such as hide-and-seek, hopscotch, and marbles. Flying kites near the coasts and jumping rope are also popular. Children who live in or near cities have toys similar to the ones found in North America. These include toy cars, trucks, airplanes, and action figures. Some children play video and computer games. Children in the countryside have fewer toys because their parents cannot afford them. However, they may have toy boats, cars, and trucks made of wood. Many children throughout the country have bicycles.

Chess is the most popular game in Colombia. It is enjoyed by adults and children. Colombians have won many South American chess contests.

Like chess, Colombians of all ages love *fútbol* (soccer). Most Colombian boys and girls play soccer for fun. Some boys dream of the chance to play for the national team when they are grown-ups. Other popular sports

Colombian children playing chess

A fútbol match

in Colombia are baseball, basketball, cycling, and boxing.

La Corrida (bullfighting) was brought to Colombia by the Spanish. Bullfighting remains popular today. Most cities and towns have rings where bullfights take place throughout the year. The most important bullfights occur in February and December. Thousands of people come to watch this dangerous sport.

Colombians who live near the coasts enjoy water sports. Fishing, scuba diving, and swimming in the Pacific Ocean and Caribbean Sea are favorite activities. Snorkeling, waterskiing, and surfing are fun, too.

Colombia's beaches are popular during the dry season.

A bird statue in San Augustín Archaeological Park

In large cities and towns, people go to the movies. Colombians see many of the same movies that are enjoyed in North America.

In the largest cities, such as Bogotá and Medellín, there are plays, concerts, and art exhibits. Crowded restaurants where bands play can be enjoyed on the weekends.

Colombians and tourists from around the world enjoy visiting San Augustín Archaeological Park, southwest of Bogotá. It has hundreds of stone statues and carvings. The carvings are of men, birds, and other animals. Some are more than five hundred years old. *Archaeologists* have found gems, necklaces, and pottery here too. A museum in the town holds many of the objects that have been discovered.

Arroz con Leche
(Milk and Rice)

In this game, children gather around in a circle holding hands. One child stands in the middle of the circle and is given the name Milk and Rice. This child runs around the inside of the circle while the other children holding hands walk around him or her. Then, Milk and Rice points to a child in the circle and sings, "With this one, yes." Then, he points to another child and sings, "With that one, no." Finally, Milk and Rice points to another child (or to the first one again) and says, "I shall marry this young girl (or young man)." The girl or boy who is chosen joins Milk and Rice in the circle. They hold hands and dance inside the circle, while the others sing "Arroz con Leche (Milk and Rice)." Then the first child joins the circle. The second child stays inside the circle and the game begins again.

Let's Celebrate!

Colombians enjoy eighteen national holidays each year. They are called *fiesta* (festival) days. Many of these days are marked with dancing, fireworks, and parades. Twelve of these festival days are religious. They include Christmas, Epiphany, and Easter.

At Christmastime, Colombians decorate their homes with Christmas trees and nativity scenes. Families and friends give each other presents. Large meals with holiday dancing and singing go on for hours. Christmas parades are held in many large cities.

In the city of Popayán, the end of the Christmas season means it is time for a two-day party. The Christmas season ends on January 6. This holiday is called the Epiphany. It marks the day the three kings visited the baby Jesus. January 5, the day before the Epiphany, is

A parade celebrating the Festival of the Whites

Musicians play during the Festival of the Whites.

called The Day of the Blacks. On this day, citizens cover their hands and faces with black shoe polish. They cover each other with it too! People dress up in costumes and wear masks. They have parades, listen to musicians, eat food, and dance in the streets and at parties.

The next day, the Epiphany, is called The Festival of the Whites. Townspeople cover themselves and others with white flour or baby powder. Strangers visiting Popayán on these days have sometimes been surprised by the unique way the citizens celebrate this fiesta.

Performers in animal costumes at the Carnaval in Barranquilla

Carnaval (Carnival) season arrives shortly after Epiphany. Carnaval is held before Lent, the forty-day period before Easter. Nearly all of Colombia celebrates Carnaval. Towns and cities hold parades with giant floats. People dress in costumes. The most famous Colombian Carnaval is held in the city of Barranquilla, on the Caribbean coast.

Corpus Christi is a Catholic festival that takes place throughout Colombia in May or June. It is a celebration of Holy Communion. People work together to make *altars*. Each group tries to make the most beautiful altar out of everyday

An Independence Day parade in Cartagena

materials, such as colored paper, cloth, and wood scraps. Flowers and candles are used to decorate them. Once they are finished, the groups parade their altars through the streets.

Independence Day is celebrated every year on July 20. It marks the beginning of Colombia's fight for independence from Spain. Schoolchildren and Colombian soldiers parade through the streets of their towns and cities. People

Women decorate a statue of their town's patron saint.

watch sports events and sing folk songs that honor Colombia. Dancers and musicians perform at night.

August 7 marks the victory of Francisco de Paula Santander's army against the Spanish. Spanish forces had retaken part of Colombia after the war for independence began. When they were defeated, Colombia became free from Spanish rule.

Some fiestas are celebrated only in certain towns, instead of throughout the country. Many of these festivals honor a town's patron saint. A patron saint is a saint who is believed to protect a town or country. One example is the festival of San Isidro that is held in the town of Río Frío. San Isidro is Saint Isidore the Farmer, who is believed to bring rain to the town. Every April 4, the people of Río Frío walk through the town behind a picture of the saint, asking him to bring rain before the festival ends.

Shouted
Christmas Presents

Children in the Cauca River valley play this game on Christmas Eve:
Two children are chosen as leaders. Each picks a team of children who are
about the same size as the leader. Everyone on the team dresses up in the same
costume. The teams come together and the leaders try to identify each other.
The trick is to do so without speaking! The first leader to succeed wins the
game. The losing team then holds a party for the winning team. Presents are
exchanged between teams at the party. Whoever is giving away a gift
shouts out the name of the person who is receiving the gift.

Colombia's flag has three stripes: yellow, blue, and red. The yellow stripe is much wider than the blue and red stripes. This is because the yellow stripe stands for Colombia's rich land. The blue stripe stands for the two oceans that border Colombia. It also stands for the country's many rivers. The red stripe is for the Colombians who fought against Spain for freedom.

The Colombian peso is Colombia's form of money. In 2003, you could receive 2,800 Colombian pesos for one U.S. dollar.

Count in Spanish

English	Spanish	Say it like this:
one	uno	OO-noh
two	dos	DOHS
three	tres	TRACE
four	cuatro	KWAH-troh
five	cinco	SEEN-koh
six	seis	SAYSS
seven	siete	see-EH-tay
eight	ocho	OH-choh
nine	nueve	NWEH-beh
ten	diez	dee-EHS

Glossary

altars   Large platforms used for worship.

archaeologists (ar-kee-OL-uh-jists)   Scientists who study the past.

artifacts   Everyday items made by people who lived long ago.

assembly   A meeting of a lot of people.

continent   One of the seven large landmasses of the Earth.

courtyard   An open area surrounded by walls.

equator (i-KWAY-tuhr)   An imaginary line around the middle of the Earth.

plantation   A large farm.

port   A town or city with a harbor where ships can dock and load or unload cargo.

thatched   Made with straw or reeds.

Fast Facts

Colombia is one of the largest countries in South America. It lies in the northwestern part of the continent.

Since Colombia borders both Central and South America, it is often called the Gateway to South America.

Three Andes mountain ranges lie side by side in Colombia. They are the Cordillera Occidental (western), the Cordillera Central, and the Cordillera Oriental (eastern).

Bogotá is Colombia's capital city. It is in the Cordillera Oriental. Bogotá is home to more than five million people.

Colombia's flag has three stripes: yellow, blue, and red. The yellow stripe stands for Colombia's rich land. The blue stripe stands for the two oceans that border Colombia. It also stands for the country's many rivers. The red stripe is for the Colombians who fought against Spain for freedom.

Spanish is Colombia's official language.

42

Ninety percent of Colombians are Roman Catholic. Catholicism is the country's official religion.

The Colombian peso is Colombia's form of money. In 2003, you could receive 2,800 Colombian pesos for one U.S. dollar.

Cristóbal Colón is the highest peak in the country. Its name is Spanish for Christopher Columbus. It stands 18,947 feet (5,775 m) high.

As of July 2002, 41,008,227 people lived in Colombia.

San Augustín Archaeological Park is southwest of Bogotá. It has hundreds of stone statues and carvings. Some are more than five hundred years old.

Chess is the most popular game in Colombia. It is enjoyed by adults and children. Colombians have won many South American chess contests.

Proud to Be Colombian

Fernando Botero (1932–   )

Fernando Botero is one of Colombia's most famous artists. He was born in Medellín in 1932. In 1951, Botero held his first art show in Bogotá. He was nineteen years old. The next year, he went to Europe to study in Spain and Italy. He returned to Bogotá in 1955, but no one seemed very interested in his work. From 1955 to 1975, Botero lived in Mexico City, New York City, and Paris. In the 1960s, people finally began to notice his art. He began exhibiting his paintings and sculptures in many countries around the world. He received many awards and honors for his work. Botero makes sculptures of children, adults, animals, and angels. They are unique because Botero's sculptures are always fat. Sometimes they look funny at first, but they often have a serious meaning.

Francisco de Paula Santander (1792–1840)

Francisco de Paula Santander was born in the town of Rosario de Cucutá. He was one of the most important leaders in the fight for independence from Spain. As a teenager, Santander was studying in Bogotá to be a lawyer. He left school to help fight for independence. He led the forces in the 1819 Battle of Boyacá. The Spanish were defeated. In 1821, Santander was made the leader of Gran Colombia. This area included present-day Colombia, Venezuela, and Ecuador. He served until 1830, when Gran Colombia was split into three separate countries. In 1832, Santander became the first elected president of Colombia.

Adriana Ocampo (1955–   )

Born in Barranquilla, Adriana Ocampo arrived in the United States when she was fifteen years old. She graduated from high school in Pasadena, California, and from the University of California at Los Angeles. Ocampo works in California at the Jet Propulsion Laboratory (JPL). The JPL is a part of NASA, the United States space agency. Ocampo studies planets. She has worked on the teams that sent the *Viking* mission to Mars, the *Voyager* mission to Uranus, Neptune, and Pluto, and the *Galileo* mission to Jupiter. She has also studied the crater that is believed to have been left by the meteor that crashed to Earth, causing the extinction of the dinosaurs. Ocampo has applied to NASA for astronaut training.

Find Out More

Books

Colombia by Tracey Boraas. Bridgestone Books, Mankato, MN, 2002.

Colombia by Leeanne Gelletly. Mason Crest Publishers, Broomall, PA, 2003.

Colombia by Caleb Owens. The Child's World, Chanhassen, MN, 2003.

The Monkey People: A Colombian Folktale by Eric Metaxas. Rabbit Ears Books, New York, 1995.

Web Site

Go to **www.colombiaemb.org** and click on the "Kids' Homework Helper" page for a lot of interesting facts—especially how to remember the correct way to spell "Colombia." There are lots of links to other Colombian sites and also a recording of Colombia's national anthem.

Videos

Full Circle with Michael Palin: Peru and Colombia. PBS Home Video, 2000.

The Monkey People. Rabbit Ears Productions, 1991.

Index

Page numbers for illustrations are in **boldface.**

About the Author

Sarah De Capua is the author of many books, including nonfiction, biographies, geography, and historical titles. She loves to travel and write about the places she has visited when she gets home. Born and raised in Connecticut, she now calls Colorado home.

Acknowledgments

My thanks to Margo Valentin for her invaluable assistance in translating some of my research from Spanish to English.